THE CROWNED LIFE

A Prayer Journal to Examine Your Heart Posture

T'Edra Z Knox

The CROWNED Life: A Prayer Journal to Examine Your Heart Posture

ISBN: 978-1-954595-12-5

Library of Congress Control Number: 2021919949

Sparkle Publishing
www.sparklepublishing.net
Printed in the USA.
Duncanville, Texas

Sparkle Publishing
Write. Publish. Sparkle.

Dedication

To my grandmother, Willie Mae Jackson, and aunts, thank you for imparting in me the power of prayer and living a life that exemplifies Christ.

To my grandfather Emmett Lee King, thank you for affirming my royal position in this world, thank you for building the confidence in my calling, the victory in my voice, and the power of my posture.

To my family, thank you all, and to my husband, Mr. Edward H Knox III, thank you for providing a haven where my posture and prayers were cultivated, covered, and supported. Thank you for your never-ending love on this CROWNED life journey.

Paul Quinn College Library thank you for reigniting the reader within and creating a space for me to discover writing as an outlet.

Table of Contents

Purpose of Journal

The CROWNED Life Prayer Journal is designed to help you analyze your heart's posture for God's purpose to prevail.

How to use your CROWNED Life Prayer Journal:

AFFIRMATION: In this section practice speaking life through positive affirmation. Say these affirmations out loud throughout your day. The words you think and act on have an impact on your posture. When you speak positive affirmations, you recognize God's ways are better, accept God's Will for your life, and act in a way that pleases Him.

SERMON NOTES: In this section, write the key points from a sermon or Bible study that will help you with the following:

Application: Putting the message into practice.

Introspection: Examining your posture.

Reflection: Seeing a true reflection of yourself.

REFLECTION QUESTIONS:

In this section, read the reflection scripture at the top of each page and answer the questions identified as the 4Cs. Answering these questions will increase your connection with Christ. The 4Cs are identified as the following: (1) Create, (2) Cover, (3) Carry, and (4) Crown.

CREATE: Are you looking at the scripture and seeing yourself reflected in it? Often, we struggle with scripture because we do not see ourselves or the obstacles within it.

COVER: This is the question where things become genuinely intimate; it is just you and God and whatever insight He has for you about your heart's posture. This question necessitates a mixture of repentance and gratitude.

CARRY: There is more to what God revealed to you than writing it down and going about your business. He is preparing you and setting you to reign and rule. The reflection question referencing "Carry" helps you be grateful for God's planning, preparing, and pruning of your heart.

CROWN: What steps can you take to apply this text to your life now that it is time to walk it out?

PRAYER REQUEST: We must learn to trust God's track record. In this section record who needs prayer, their prayer requests, and God's response to your prayers. Recording how God responds to your prayers will give you hope and receipts to show you how God is genuinely concerned about helping His people.

Introduction

This journal provides women of faith a tool to establish a deeper connection with God, our Creator. It will provide introspection on your relationships with yourself and others. As you reflect daily, you will begin to see how the posture of your heart affects all areas of your life. The posture of our prayers is vital to our relationship with God and with those we encounter daily. Constant examination of our posture allows us to understand why we do the things we do.

I Am
CROWNED.

Sermon Notes

Date: _____

Pastor/Speaker: _____

Title: _____

Notes: _____

_____

_____

_____

_____

_____

_____

_____

_____

_____

_____

_____

_____

Cast all your anxiety on him because he cares for you.
1 Peter 5:7

Created: How did I identify with this scripture?

_____

_____

_____

Cover: What did this scripture reveal to me?

_____

_____

_____

Carry: How can this scripture prepare me for my purpose?

_____

_____

_____

Crown: How can I apply this scripture to my life?

_____

_____

_____

Name	Prayer Request	God's Outcome?

Execute in the Spirit in Excellence.

Sermon Notes

Date: _____

Pastor/Speaker: _____

Title: _____

Notes: _____

_____

_____

_____

_____

_____

_____

_____

_____

_____

_____

_____

_____

So be truly glad. There is wonderful joy ahead, even though you must endure many trials for a little while.
1 Peter 1:6

Created: How did I identify with this scripture?

_____

_____

_____

Cover: What did this scripture reveal to me?

_____

_____

_____

Carry: How can this scripture prepare me for my purpose?

_____

_____

_____

Crown: How can I apply this scripture to my life?

_____

_____

_____

Name	Prayer Request	God's Outcome?

I Am More Than Qualified to Be Here.

Sermon Notes

Date: _____

Pastor/Speaker: _____

Title: _____

Notes:_____

_____

_____

_____

_____

_____

_____

_____

_____

_____

_____

_____

_____

For wisdom will enter your heart, and knowledge
will fill you with joy.
Proverbs 2:10

Created: How did I identify with this scripture?

_____

_____

_____

Cover: What did this scripture reveal to me?

_____

_____

_____

Carry: How can this scripture prepare me for my purpose?

_____

_____

_____

Crown: How can I apply this scripture to my life?

_____

_____

_____

Name	Prayer Request	God's Outcome?

I Will Not Compete with My Calling.

Sermon Notes

Date: _____

Pastor/Speaker: _____

Title: _____

Notes: _____

_____

_____

_____

_____

_____

_____

_____

_____

_____

_____

_____

_____

Enthusiasm without knowledge is no good;
haste makes mistakes.
Proverbs 19:2

Created: How did I identify with this scripture?

_____

_____

_____

Cover: What did this scripture reveal to me?

_____

_____

_____

Carry: How can this scripture prepare me for my purpose?

_____

_____

_____

Crown: How can I apply this scripture to my life?

_____

_____

_____

Name	Prayer Request	God's Outcome?

Proceed With Confidence.

Sermon Notes

Date: _____

Pastor/Speaker: _____

Title: _____

Notes: _____

_____

_____

_____

_____

_____

_____

_____

_____

_____

_____

_____

_____

_____

For our present troubles are small and won't last very long.
Yet they produce for us a glory that vastly outweighs them
and will last forever!
2 Corinthians 4:17

Created: How did I identify with this scripture?

_____

_____

_____

Cover: What did this scripture reveal to me?

_____

_____

_____

Carry: How can this scripture prepare me for my purpose?

_____

_____

_____

Crown: How can I apply this scripture to my life?

_____

_____

_____

Name	Prayer Request	God's Outcome?

I Give Myself Permission to Evolve.

Sermon Notes

Date: _____

Pastor/Speaker: _____

Title: _____

Notes: _____

_____

_____

_____

_____

_____

_____

_____

_____

_____

_____

_____

_____

Too much talk leads to sin.
Be sensible and keep your mouth shut.
Proverbs 10:19

Created: How did I identify with this scripture?

_____

_____

_____

Cover: What did this scripture reveal to me?

_____

_____

_____

Carry: How can this scripture prepare me for my purpose?

_____

_____

_____

Crown: How can I apply this scripture to my life?

_____

_____

_____

Name	Prayer Request	God's Outcome?

Progress Over Perfection.

Sermon Notes

Date: _____

Pastor/Speaker: _____

Title: _____

Notes: _____

_____

_____

_____

_____

_____

_____

_____

_____

_____

_____

_____

_____

And what do you benefit if you gain the whole world but lose
your own soul?
Mark 8:36

Created: How did I identify with this scripture?

_____

_____

_____

Cover: What did this scripture reveal to me?

_____

_____

_____

Carry: How can this scripture prepare me for my purpose?

_____

_____

_____

Crown: How can I apply this scripture to my life?

_____

_____

_____

Name	Prayer Request	God's Outcome?

Don't Diminish Your Destiny.

Sermon Notes

Date: _____

Pastor/Speaker: _____

Title: _____

Notes: _____

_____

_____

_____

_____

_____

_____

_____

_____

_____

_____

_____

The Lord is my shepherd, I lack nothing.
Psalm 23:1

Created: How did I identify with this scripture?

_____

_____

_____

Cover: What did this scripture reveal to me?

_____

_____

_____

Carry: How can this scripture prepare me for my purpose?

_____

_____

_____

Crown: How can I apply this scripture to my life?

_____

_____

_____

Name	Prayer Request	God's Outcome?

Different Doesn't Mean Diminished.

Sermon Notes

Date: _____

Pastor/Speaker: _____

Title: _____

Notes: _____

_____

_____

_____

_____

_____

_____

_____

_____

_____

_____

_____

_____

Wise choices will watch over you.
Understanding will keep you safe.
Proverbs 2:11

Created: How did I identify with this scripture?

_____

_____

_____

Cover: What did this scripture reveal to me?

_____

_____

_____

Carry: How can this scripture prepare me for my purpose?

_____

_____

_____

Crown: How can I apply this scripture to my life?

_____

_____

_____

Name	Prayer Request	God's Outcome?

Different Is
Distinguished.

Sermon Notes

Date: _____

Pastor/Speaker: _____

Title: _____

Notes: _____

_____

_____

_____

_____

_____

_____

_____

_____

_____

_____

_____

Seek the kingdom of God above all else and live righteously
and he will give you everything you need.
Matthew 6:33

Created: How did I identify with this scripture?

_____

_____

_____

Cover: What did this scripture reveal to me?

_____

_____

_____

Carry: How can this scripture prepare me for my purpose?

_____

_____

_____

Crown: How can I apply this scripture to my life?

_____

_____

_____

Name	Prayer Request	God's Outcome?

I Will Own and Honor My Crown in This Season.

Sermon Notes

Date: _____

Pastor/Speaker: _____

Title: _____

Notes: _____

_____

_____

_____

_____

_____

_____

_____

_____

_____

_____

_____

_____

Love each other with genuine affection and take delight in honoring each other.
Romans 12:10

Created: How did I identify with this scripture?

_____

_____

_____

Cover: What did this scripture reveal to me?

_____

_____

_____

Carry: How can this scripture prepare me for my purpose?

_____

_____

_____

Crown: How can I apply this scripture to my life?

_____

_____

_____

Name	Prayer Request	God's Outcome?

I Am God's Representative.

Sermon Notes

Date: _____

Pastor/Speaker: _____

Title: _____

Notes: _____

_____

_____

_____

_____

_____

_____

_____

_____

_____

_____

_____

_____

If one part suffers, all the parts suffer with it, and if one part is honored, all the parts are glad.
1 Corinthians 12:26

Created: How did I identify with this scripture?

_____

_____

_____

Cover: What did this scripture reveal to me?

_____

_____

_____

Carry: How can this scripture prepare me for my purpose?

_____

_____

_____

Crown: How can I apply this scripture to my life?

_____

_____

_____

Name	Prayer Request	God's Outcome?

The World Will Always Catch Up with God's Word.

Sermon Notes

Date: _____

Pastor/Speaker: _____

Title: _____

Notes: _____

_____

_____

_____

_____

_____

_____

_____

_____

_____

_____

_____

_____

_____

These were his instructions to them: "The harvest is great, but the workers are few. So, pray to the Lord who is in charge of the harvest; ask him to send more workers into his field.
Luke 10:2

Created: How did I identify with this scripture?

_____

_____

_____

Cover: What did this scripture reveal to me?

_____

_____

_____

Carry: How can this scripture prepare me for my purpose?

_____

_____

_____

Crown: How can I apply this scripture to my life?

_____

_____

_____

Name	Prayer Request	God's Outcome?

No Need to Compete or Compare When God Has Already CROWNED Me.

Sermon Notes

Date: _____

Pastor/Speaker: _____

Title: _____

Notes:_____

_____

_____

_____

_____

_____

_____

_____

_____

_____

_____

_____

_____

_____

Even though I walk through the darkest valley, I will fear no evil, for you are with me; your rod and your staff, they comfort me.
Psalm 23:4

Created: How did I identify with this scripture?

_____

_____

_____

Cover: What did this scripture reveal to me?

_____

_____

_____

Carry: How can this scripture prepare me for my purpose?

_____

_____

_____

Crown: How can I apply this scripture to my life?

_____

_____

_____

Name	Prayer Request	God's Outcome?

I Am the Kingsskid.

Sermon Notes

Date: _____

Pastor/Speaker: _____

Title: _____

Notes: _____

_____

_____

_____

_____

_____

_____

_____

_____

_____

_____

_____

_____

Let us not become conceited, or provoke one another, or be jealous of one another.
Galatians 5:26

Created: How did I identify with this scripture?

_____

_____

_____

Cover: What did this scripture reveal to me?

_____

_____

_____

Carry: How can this scripture prepare me for my purpose?

_____

_____

_____

Crown: How can I apply this scripture to my life?

_____

_____

_____

Name	Prayer Request	God's Outcome?

Walk In Wisdom.

Sermon Notes

Date: _____

Pastor/Speaker: _____

Title: _____

Notes: _____

_____

_____

_____

_____

_____

_____

_____

_____

_____

_____

_____

_____

The human body has many parts, but the many parts make up one whole body. So, it is with the body of Christ.
1 Corinthians 12:12

Created: How did I identify with this scripture?

_____

_____

_____

Cover: What did this scripture reveal to me?

_____

_____

_____

Carry: How can this scripture prepare me for my purpose?

_____

_____

_____

Crown: How can I apply this scripture to my life?

_____

_____

_____

Name	Prayer Request	God's Outcome?

Don't Let the Rain of This Season Keep You from Reigning in Life.

Sermon Notes

Date: _____

Pastor/Speaker: _____

Title: _____

Notes: _____

_____

_____

_____

_____

_____

_____

_____

_____

_____

_____

_____

_____

Then Christ will make his home in your hearts as you trust in
him. Your roots will grow down into
God's love and keep you strong.
Ephesians 3:17

Created: How did I identify with this scripture?

_____

_____

_____

Cover: What did this scripture reveal to me?

_____

_____

_____

Carry: How can this scripture prepare me for my purpose?

_____

_____

_____

Crown: How can I apply this scripture to my life?

_____

_____

_____

Name	Prayer Request	God's Outcome?

Some Say When It Rains; It Pours, I Say When I Reign, I Rule.

Sermon Notes

Date: _____

Pastor/Speaker: _____

Title: _____

Notes: _____

_____

_____

_____

_____

_____

_____

_____

_____

_____

_____

_____

_____

Look straight ahead and fix your eyes
on what lies before you.
Proverbs 4:25

Created: How did I identify with this scripture?

_____

_____

_____

Cover: What did this scripture reveal to me?

_____

_____

_____

Carry: How can this scripture prepare me for my purpose?

_____

_____

_____

Crown: How can I apply this scripture to my life?

_____

_____

_____

Name	Prayer Request	God's Outcome?

Maintain Peace.

Sermon Notes

Date: _____

Pastor/Speaker: _____

Title: _____

Notes: _____

_____

_____

_____

_____

_____

_____

_____

_____

_____

_____

_____

_____

Three things will last forever—faith, hope, and love—and the greatest of these is love.
1 Corinthians 13:13

Created: How did I identify with this scripture?

_____

_____

_____

Cover: What did this scripture reveal to me?

_____

_____

_____

Carry: How can this scripture prepare me for my purpose?

_____

_____

_____

Crown: How can I apply this scripture to my life?

_____

_____

_____

Name	Prayer Request	God's Outcome?

There Is Victory in Your Voice.

Sermon Notes

Date: _____

Pastor/Speaker: _____

Title: _____

Notes: _____

_____

_____

_____

_____

_____

_____

_____

_____

_____

_____

_____

_____

_____

Trust in the Lord with all your heart; do not
depend on your own understanding.
Proverbs 3:5

Created: How did I identify with this scripture?

_____

_____

_____

Cover: What did this scripture reveal to me?

_____

_____

_____

Carry: How can this scripture prepare me for my purpose?

_____

_____

_____

Crown: How can I apply this scripture to my life?

_____

_____

_____

Name	Prayer Request	God's Outcome?

I Won't Be Anxious.

Sermon Notes

Date: _____

Pastor/Speaker: _____

Title: _____

Notes: _____

_____

_____

_____

_____

_____

_____

_____

_____

_____

_____

_____

Avoid all perverse talk; stay away from corrupt speech.
Proverbs 4:24

Created: How did I identify with this scripture?

_____

_____

_____

Cover: What did this scripture reveal to me?

_____

_____

_____

Carry: How can this scripture prepare me for my purpose?

_____

_____

_____

Crown: How can I apply this scripture to my life?

_____

_____

_____

Name	Prayer Request	God's Outcome?

I Move with Expectation!

Sermon Notes

Date: _____

Pastor/Speaker: _____

Title: _____

Notes: _____

_____

_____

_____

_____

_____

_____

_____

_____

_____

_____

_____

_____

Love never gives up, never loses faith, is always hopeful,
and endures through every circumstance.
1 Corinthians 13:7

Created: How did I identify with this scripture?

_____

_____

_____

Cover: What did this scripture reveal to me?

_____

_____

_____

Carry: How can this scripture prepare me for my purpose?

_____

_____

_____

Crown: How can I apply this scripture to my life?

_____

_____

_____

Name	Prayer Request	God's Outcome?

Enjoy The Jewels on The Journey.

Sermon Notes

Date: _____

Pastor/Speaker: _____

Title: _____

Notes: _____

_____

_____

_____

_____

_____

_____

_____

_____

_____

_____

_____

_____

_____

_____

Charm is deceptive, and beauty does not last; but a woman who fears the Lord will be greatly praised.
Proverbs 31:30

Created: How did I identify with this scripture?

_____

_____

_____

Cover: What did this scripture reveal to me?

_____

_____

_____

Carry: How can this scripture prepare me for my purpose?

_____

_____

_____

Crown: How can I apply this scripture to my life?

_____

_____

_____

Name	Prayer Request	God's Outcome?

Remember Your Why.

Sermon Notes

Date: _____

Pastor/Speaker: _____

Title: _____

Notes: _____

_____

_____

_____

_____

_____

_____

_____

_____

_____

_____

_____

_____

Now go and remember that I am sending you
out as lambs among wolves.
Luke 10:3

Created: How did I identify with this scripture?

_____

_____

_____

Cover: What did this scripture reveal to me?

_____

_____

_____

Carry: How can this scripture prepare me for my purpose?

_____

_____

_____

Crown: How can I apply this scripture to my life?

_____

_____

_____

Name	Prayer Request	God's Outcome?

I Was Created for This!

Sermon Notes

Date: _____

Pastor/Speaker: _____

Title: _____

Notes: _____

_____

_____

_____

_____

_____

_____

_____

_____

_____

_____

_____

_____

_____

All of you together are Christ's body,
and each of you is a part of it.
1 Corinthians 12:27

Created: How did I identify with this scripture?

_____

_____

_____

Cover: What did this scripture reveal to me?

_____

_____

_____

Carry: How can this scripture prepare me for my purpose?

_____

_____

_____

Crown: How can I apply this scripture to my life?

_____

_____

_____

Name	Prayer Request	God's Outcome?

I Am an Overcomer.

Sermon Notes

Date: _____

Pastor/Speaker: _____

Title: _____

Notes: _____

_____

_____

_____

_____

_____

_____

_____

_____

_____

_____

_____

_____

She carefully watches everything in her household and
suffers nothing from laziness.
Proverbs 31:27

Created: How did I identify with this scripture?

_____

_____

_____

Cover: What did this scripture reveal to me?

_____

_____

_____

Carry: How can this scripture prepare me for my purpose?

_____

_____

_____

Crown: How can I apply this scripture to my life?

_____

_____

_____

Name	Prayer Request	God's Outcome?

I Am in Alignment with My God Given Assignment.

Sermon Notes

Date: _____

Pastor/Speaker: _____

Title: _____

Notes: _____

_____

_____

_____

_____

_____

_____

_____

_____

_____

_____

_____

_____

Let perseverance finish its work so that you may be mature
and complete, not lacking anything.
James 1:4

Created: How did I identify with this scripture?

_____

_____

_____

Cover: What did this scripture reveal to me?

_____

_____

_____

Carry: How can this scripture prepare me for my purpose?

_____

_____

_____

Crown: How can I apply this scripture to my life?

_____

_____

_____

Name	Prayer Request	God's Outcome?

Maintain Focus.

Sermon Notes

Date: _____

Pastor/Speaker: _____

Title: _____

Notes: _____

_____

_____

_____

_____

_____

_____

_____

_____

_____

_____

_____

_____

These trials will show that your faith is genuine. It is being tested as fire tests and purifies gold though your faith is far more precious than mere gold. So when your faith remains strong through many trials, it will bring you much praise and glory and honor on the day when Jesus Christ is revealed to the whole world.
1 Peter 1:7

Created: How did I identify with this scripture?

_____

_____

Cover: What did this scripture reveal to me?

_____

_____

Carry: How can this scripture prepare me for my purpose?

_____

_____

Crown: How can I apply this scripture to my life?

_____

_____

Name	Prayer Request	God's Outcome?

My Identity
Is in God.

Sermon Notes

Date: _____

Pastor/Speaker: _____

Title: _____

Notes: _____

_____

_____

_____

_____

_____

_____

_____

_____

_____

_____

_____

_____

_____

Because you know that the testing of
your faith produces perseverance.
James 1:3

Created: How did I identify with this scripture?

_____

_____

_____

Cover: What did this scripture reveal to me?

_____

_____

_____

Carry: How can this scripture prepare me for my purpose?

_____

_____

_____

Crown: How can I apply this scripture to my life?

_____

_____

_____

Name	Prayer Request	God's Outcome?

Love Never Fails.

Sermon Notes

Date: _____

Pastor/Speaker: _____

Title: _____

Notes: _____

_____

_____

_____

_____

_____

_____

_____

_____

_____

_____

_____

Consider it pure joy, my brothers and sisters, whenever you face trials of many kinds.

James 1:2

Created: How did I identify with this scripture?

_____

_____

_____

Cover: What did this scripture reveal to me?

_____

_____

_____

Carry: How can this scripture prepare me for my purpose?

_____

_____

_____

Crown: How can I apply this scripture to my life?

_____

_____

_____

Name	Prayer Request	God's Outcome?

Praise Activates God's Power.

Sermon Notes

Date: _____

Pastor/Speaker: _____

Title: _____

Notes: _____

_____

_____

_____

_____

_____

_____

_____

_____

_____

_____

_____

_____

As Jesus and the disciples continued on their way to Jerusalem, they came to a certain village where a woman named Martha welcomed him into her home. 39 Her sister, Mary, sat at the Lord's feet, listening to what he taught. 40 But Martha was distracted by the big dinner she was preparing. She came to Jesus and said, "Lord, doesn't it seem unfair to you that my sister just sits here while I do all the work? Tell her to come and help me."

41 But the Lord said to her, "My dear Martha, you are worried and upset over all these details! 42 There is only one thing worth being concerned about. Mary has discovered it, and it will not be taken away from her."

Luke 10:38-42

Created: How did I identify with this scripture?

_____

_____

_____

Cover: What did this scripture reveal to me?

_____

_____

_____

Carry: How can this scripture prepare me for my purpose?

_____

_____

_____

Crown: How can I apply this scripture to my life?

_____

_____

_____

Name	Prayer Request	God's Outcome?

Be Still.

Sermon Notes

Date: _____

Pastor/Speaker: _____

Title: _____

Notes: _____

_____

_____

_____

_____

_____

_____

_____

_____

_____

_____

_____

_____

May he grant your heart's desires and
make all your plans succeed.
Psalm 20:4

Created: How did I identify with this scripture?

_____

_____

_____

Cover: What did this scripture reveal to me?

_____

_____

_____

Carry: How can this scripture prepare me for my purpose?

_____

_____

_____

Crown: How can I apply this scripture to my life?

_____

_____

_____

Name	Prayer Request	God's Outcome?

Be Willing.

Sermon Notes

Date: _____

Pastor/Speaker: _____

Title: _____

Notes: _____

_____

_____

_____

_____

_____

_____

_____

_____

_____

_____

_____

_____

When she speaks, her words are wise, and she gives
instructions with kindness.
Proverbs 31:26

Created: How did I identify with this scripture?

_____

_____

_____

Cover: What did this scripture reveal to me?

_____

_____

_____

Carry: How can this scripture prepare me for my purpose?

_____

_____

_____

Crown: How can I apply this scripture to my life?

_____

_____

_____

Name	Prayer Request	God's Outcome?

Gossip The Gospel.

Sermon Notes

Date: _____

Pastor/Speaker: _____

Title: _____

Notes: _____

_____

_____

_____

_____

_____

_____

_____

_____

_____

_____

_____

_____

_____

Don't repay evil for evil. Don't retaliate with insults when people insult you. Instead, pay them back with a blessing. That is what God has called you to do, and he will grant you his blessing.
1 Peter 3:9

Created: How did I identify with this scripture?

_____

_____

Cover: What did this scripture reveal to me?

_____

_____

Carry: How can this scripture prepare me for my purpose?

_____

_____

Crown: How can I apply this scripture to my life?

_____

_____

Name	Prayer Request	God's Outcome?

I Dominate in
My Destiny.

Sermon Notes

Date: _____

Pastor/Speaker: _____

Title: _____

Notes: _____

_____

_____

_____

_____

_____

_____

_____

_____

_____

_____

_____

_____

Discover your identity in God
Trust his track record
Live the CROWNED Life

Then the eleven disciples left for Galilee, going to the mountain where Jesus had told them to go. 17 When they saw him, they worshiped him—but some of them doubted!18 Jesus came and told his disciples, "I have been given all authority in heaven and on earth. 19 Therefore, go and make disciples of all the nations, baptizing them in the name of the Father and the Son and the Holy Spirit. 20 Teach these new disciples to obey all the commands I have given you. And be sure of this: I am with you always, even to the end of the age.

Matthew 28:16-20

Created: How did I identify with this scripture?

_____

_____

_____

Cover: What did this scripture reveal to me?

_____

_____

_____

Carry: How can this scripture prepare me for my purpose?

_____

_____

_____

Crown: How can I apply this scripture to my life?

_____

_____

_____

Name	Prayer Request	God's Outcome?

Stay CROWNED with T'Edra

 Kingsskid

 Kingsskid

 www.kingsskid.com

 tedra@kingsskid.com

Made in the USA
Columbia, SC
13 January 2022